BASIC BIOGRAPHIES

Rosa Parks

by Cynthia Amoroso and Robert B. Noyed

Rosa Parks was a very brave woman. All her life, she wanted people to be treated fairly.

Rosa Parks worked toward fairness for all people.

Rosa was born in Alabama on February 4, 1913. She grew up in the town of Pine Level.

Rosa lived in Alabama for many years.

When Rosa was growing up, the laws for black people were different from the laws for white people. Many places were "whites only." Black people could not go there.

Signs told white people and black people to use separate areas.

On buses, black people had to sit in the back. If whites wanted to sit on a full bus, blacks always had to give up their seats.

Black people had to sit at the back of buses.

One day in Montgomery, Alabama, Rosa was riding on a full bus. A white person wanted her seat.

This black woman would have to give up her seat if a white person wanted it.

The bus driver told Rosa to give up her seat. Rosa did not move. The police took her off the bus. Rosa was **arrested**.

Rosa was taken to the police station.

Rosa's friends were angry. Black people decided not to ride the buses in Montgomery until the law was changed.

No black people rode the buses until the law changed.

A year later, the law changed. Black people could not be treated in such an unfair way. All people now had the same **rights** on the bus.

The law changed in 1956, so anyone could sit at the front of a bus.

Rosa's actions **inspired** people. Soon people across the country were working for equal rights.

People marched for equal rights in Washington DC in 1963.

Rosa kept working to make life better for all people. She died in 2005. People remember how Rosa worked to make things fair.

This is Rosa at age 75. She lived to be 92 years old.

Glossary

arrested (uh–REST-id): A person who is arrested is taken to jail by the police. Rosa was arrested for staying in her seat on a bus.

inspired (in–SPYRD): To be inspired is to be encouraged to feel a certain way or take a certain action. Rosa inspired others to work for fairness.

rights (RITES): Rights are things people are allowed to do. Rosa worked for equal rights.

To Find Out More

Books

Clay, Wil, Jim Haskins, and Rosa Parks. *I Am Rosa Parks*. New York: Puffin, 2000.

Mara, Wil. *Rosa Parks*. Danbury, CT: Children's Press, 2007.

Ringgold, Faith. *If A Bus Could Talk: The Story of Rosa Parks*. New York: Simon, 2003.

Web Sites

Visit our Web site for links about Rosa Parks: *childsworld.com/links*

Note to Parents, Teachers, and Librarians: We routinely verify our Web links to make sure they are safe and active sites. So encourage your readers to check them out!

Index

About the Authors

Cynthia Amoroso has worked as an elementary school teacher and a high school English teacher. Writing children's books is another way for her to share her passion for the written word.

Robert B. Noyed has worked as a newspaper reporter and in the communications department for a Minnesota school district. He enjoys the challenge and accomplishment of writing children's books.

On the cover: Rosa Parks went to court in 1956.

Published by The Child's World®
1980 Lookout Drive • Mankato, MN 56003-1705
800-599-READ • www.childsworld.com

ACKNOWLEDGMENTS
The Child's World®: Mary Berendes, Publishing Director
The Design Lab: Design and production
Red Line Editorial: Editorial direction

PHOTO CREDITS: AP Images, cover, 5, 7, 11, 17, 19; Rich Koele/iStockphoto, cover, 1, 16, 22; Gene Herrick/iStockphoto, 3, 13; Horace Cort/AP Images, 9, 15; Michael J. Samojeden/AP Images, 21

Printed in the United States of America in Mankato, Minnesota.
November 2009
F11460

LIBRARY OF CONGRESS CATALOGING-IN-PUBLICATION DATA
Amoroso, Cynthia.
  Rosa Parks / by Cynthia Amoroso and Robert B. Noyed.
    p. cm. — (Basic biographies)
  Includes index.
  ISBN 978-1-60253-344-8 (library bound : alk. paper)
  1. Parks, Rosa, 1913-2005—Juvenile literature. 2. African American women civil rights workers—Alabama—Montgomery—Biography—Juvenile literature. 3. African Americans—Alabama—Montgomery—Biography—Juvenile literature. 4. Civil rights workers—Alabama—Montgomery—Biography—Juvenile literature. 5. African Americans—Civil rights—Alabama—Montgomery—History--20th century—Juvenile literature. 6. Segregation in transportation—Alabama—Montgomery—History—20th century—Juvenile literature. 7. Montgomery (Ala.)—Race relations—Juvenile literature.
  8. Montgomery (Ala.)—Biography—Juvenile literature. I. Noyed, Robert B. II. Title.
  F334.M753P3716 2009
  323.092—dc22   2009029372